IMAGES
of America

HARRIMAN STATE PARK

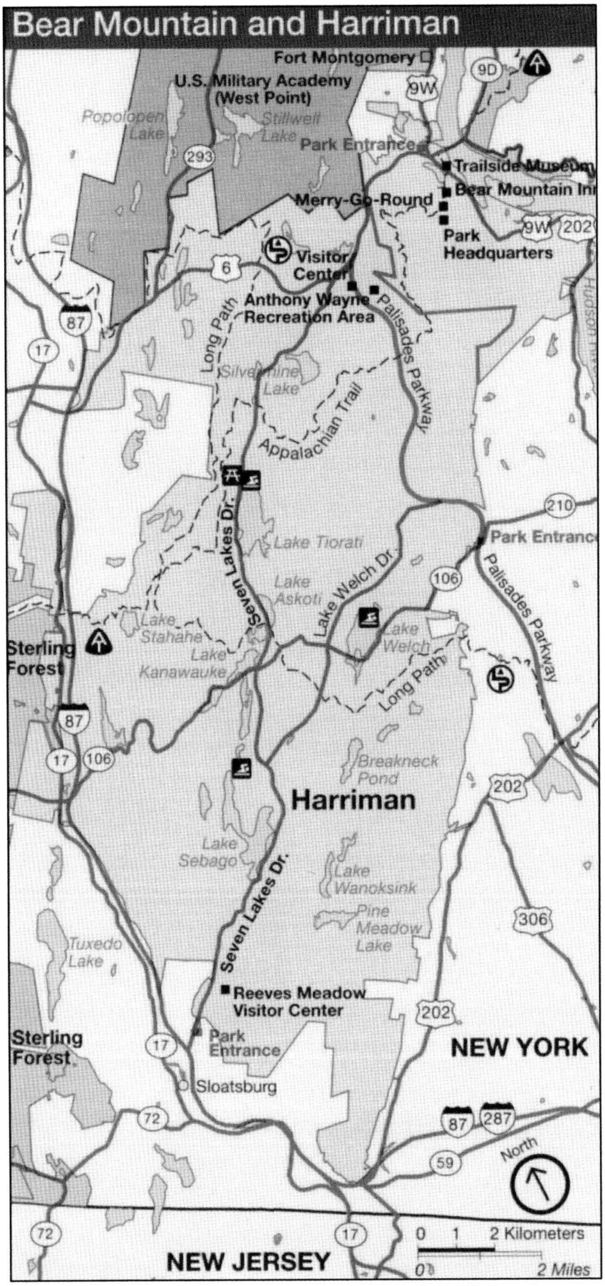

Park Map. Measuring roughly 15 miles from north to south and 5 miles east to west, Harriman State Park encompasses over 46,000 acres of forests, lakes, meadows, swamps, and streams. Conveniently reached by several highways, the park offers hiking, swimming, boating, fishing, camping, beauty, and peace. (Palisades Interstate Park Commission.)

On the Cover: Five happy campers in fashionable woolen bathing suits and beach shoes carry their canoe to the edge of the Camp Onika dock in anticipation of a lovely day at Lake Cohasset around 1923. From the 1920s to the present, the lakes of Harriman State Park have been the sites of dozens of recreational camps. (Palisades Interstate Park Commission.)

IMAGES
of America

HARRIMAN STATE PARK

Ronnie Clark Coffey

ARCADIA
PUBLISHING

ISBN 978-0-7385-7293-2

Published by Arcadia Publishing
Charleston, South Carolina

Printed in the United States of America

Library of Congress Control Number: 2009939874

For all general information contact Arcadia Publishing at:
Telephone 843-853-2070
Fax 843-853-0044
E-mail sales@arcadiapublishing.com
For customer service and orders:
Toll-Free 1-888-313-2665

Visit us on the Internet at www.arcadiapublishing.com

LAKE SCENE. The tranquility of two rowboats moving across a picturesque lake is typical of Harriman State Park. Visible at left are the waterfront and dock at Camp Yonkers on Upper Twin Lake that operated from 1921 to 1959. On the hill in the distance are two other camps. (Palisades Interstate Park Commission.)

CONTENTS

ACKNOWLEDGMENTS

The history of Harriman State Park has been preserved in numerous places. Among them are the annual reports and photographic archives of the Palisades Interstate Park Commission, the vertical files of local historical societies and libraries, long out-of-print books loaned by friends, and the precious albums and memories of individuals whose connections to the park go back for decades. In writing this book, I was fortunate to have been given access to all of these.

Regarding my research, I begin by thanking Susan Smith, restoration and development director of the Palisades Interstate Park Commission (PIPC), for access to its extensive archives, particularly the photograph collection documented by Robert Wallace, and for also answering my questions and checking and editing my manuscript. Edwin McGowan, director of science and Trailside Museums, was instrumental in arranging my use of the archives. All images not otherwise attributed were loaned for publication by the PIPC. Several organizations and institutions were extremely helpful with my research. They are the Historical Society of the Palisades Interstate Park Region, Franklin D. Roosevelt Library, Library of Congress, and the New York-New Jersey Trail Conference.

Through the generosity of Jaqueline Schassler Aguanno, Kenneth Conklin, Claire Odell Schaper, Elizabeth "Perk" Stalter, and Georgia Wallace, I was able to use images from their private collections. Special thanks go to Suzanne Brahm and the staff of the Highland Falls Library. I am indebted to the following individuals who shared time, memories and information with me: Linda Alvira, Florence Anderson, William Bailey, Norman Brahm, Bart Brooks, Peter Carroll, James Donnery, Stuart Chaney, Jack Focht, Michelle Figliomeni, Chris Ingui, Judy Kesselman, Peter Olivia, Susan Scher, Kelly Wallace Stang, and Richard Vacek. I relied heavily on the research done by William Myles for his book *Harriman Trails*, a must-have for anyone exploring the park. Likewise I benefitted from Robert Binnewiess's fascinating history, *Palisades: 100,000 in 100 Years.* Finally I am deeply grateful for the help and loving support of my husband, Kevin. My daughters Veronica and Juliet, as always, offered their humor and encouragement.

—Ronnie Clark Coffey
January 2010

INTRODUCTION

In the wilderness is the preservation of the world.
—Henry David Thoreau

Less than a one hour drive from New York City, straddling Orange and Rockland Counties, is Harriman State Park, a wilderness stretching for 15 miles from north to south and 5 miles from east to west. Within these more than 46,000 acres, there are mountains, lakes, ponds, streams, swamps, woodland animals, numerous bird species, and the remains of human endeavor from Native Americans to miners to mid-20th-century communities. That this huge parcel of the Hudson Highlands was preserved from development is remarkable. Its existence is owed largely to Edward H. and Mary Harriman whose generous gift of their own land became the original park.

During the late 19th century, as the urban sprawl of New York City spread outward, lovers of mountains and woods were filled with concern. As explained by William Myers in Harriman Trails, "The Hudson Highlands and the Palisades of the Hudson were a much admired feature of American landscape . . . they were also much admired by quarrymen who, after 1875, used Alfred Nobel's dynamite to destroy the cliffs. Between New Jersey and New York there were 17 quarries." Conservationists advocated for a national forest preserve on both sides of the Hudson. In response to the call for preservation of the scenery, Palisades Interstate Park Commission (PIPC) came into being. Under the direction of George W. Perkins, the PIPC stopped the systematic destruction of the Palisades.

Problems, however, developed further north. In 1908, New York's prison commission made plans to close Sing Sing Prison and construct a new one at Bear Mountain. They planned to put the prisoners to work by quarrying traprock from the mountain and the nearby Hudson River bank. One of those alarmed by the relocation of the prison was Edward Henry Harriman, owner of thousands of acres adjacent to the Bear Mountain tract. Harriman, a railroad magnate, had accumulated his considerable wealth through his controlling interests in the Union Pacific, Southern Pacific, and Illinois Central Railroads. His concern over the seemingly inevitable destruction of the Highlands had led him to privately purchase land in order to protect it. He proposed to donate thousands of acres of his estate as well as $1 million to the PIPC on the condition that the State of New York discontinued work on the prison and provided matching funds to expand the park to the Hudson River. Although Harriman died in 1909, his wife, Mary, and son, William Averell, carried out his wishes. In October 1910, the Harriman donation became Harriman State Park and the State of New York gave jurisdiction of the former prison site at Bear Mountain to the PIPC to become Bear Mountain State Park.

Bear Mountain and Harriman State Parks are thus adjacent properties with separate boundaries, Harriman being nine times larger. Closer to the Hudson, Bear Mountain became the more heavily trafficked site, popular with day visitors. But the trails and camps of Harriman were ideal for those seeking more of a wilderness experience.

The focus of this book is the history and development of Harriman State Park. Under the auspices of Maj. William A. Welch, general manager and chief landscape engineer of the PIPC from 1912 to 1940, major construction projects were envisioned and accomplished, including the Seven Lakes Drive, 14 lakes and dams, over 100 camps, and numerous trails. The most famous of these trails was the first segment of the Appalachian Trail. Each year saw improvements, such as sturdy trail shelters, fire towers, a ski slope, and interior roads. A major focus of the park was to provide camps and nature education for city youth, and an array of projects supported this endeavor.

The expansion and development of the park, however, had its cost. The PIPC had a strong desire to enlarge the park to preserve as much land as possible and further unite the Harriman and Bear Mountain properties. Every year more land was purchased from farmers living in or near the parkland. At first, the acquisition involved willing sellers, but later the PIPC used its power of eminent domain to force landowners to leave. Sadness and loss are still felt by some descendants of those who unwillingly left their homesteads.

After World War II, construction started on the Palisades Interstate Parkway linking the New Jersey section to the north and making Harriman State Park more accessible to motorists. The Anthony Wayne Recreation Area and Lake Welch Beach opened to accommodate postwar visitors. Through the years, budget cuts have eliminated some activities, including the Silvermine ski slope, roller skating rinks, and the pools at Anthony Wayne; however, Harriman State Park remains true to its original mission of providing a wilderness experience for those seeking an escape from urban areas. Summer days find its lakes filled with bathers, traversed by fishermen and kayakers, and its camps ringing with the laughter of children. Counselors at nature museums reveal the mysteries of woodland creatures to young visitors. Families on day outings, scouts on weekend trips, and through-hikers on the Appalachian Trail or the Long Path utilize the trails. Roadways are busy with automobiles, bicycles, and motorcycles. Reflecting on the creation of this majestic, mountainous, forested park so close to New York City, one can concur with the words of Pres. Theodore Roosevelt, himself a protector of more than 230 million acres of parkland: "There is a delight in the hardy life of the open. There are no words that can tell the hidden spirit of the wilderness that can reveal its mystery, its melancholy and its charm. The nation behaves well if it treats the natural resources as assets which it must turn over to the next generation."

One

Roots

Take any trail into the towering forests of Harriman State Park and one will encounter roots of every variety. At one's feet are the gnarled roots of oak, ash, and hemlock trees like those that sheltered the Native Americans who hunted and gathered here from about 10,000 BCE to the encounter with Europeans known as the Historic Contact period. They were of Algonquian cultural lineage, belonging to the Munsee-speaking group of Lenape-Delaware Indians. Walk further along the path and one may notice the roots of flowering trees, lilac, and wisteria and berry bushes planted by early settlers to shade porches or provide a family with fruit. Now overgrown, exposed, twisted roots sometimes conceal stone foundations of long abandoned cabins of woodcutters or entwine the entrances of iron mines that were worked diligently for 100 years. Iron mining and its support industries of woodcutting, charcoal production, and carting have drawn people to these hills.

Unearthed from beneath the roots, archeologists have found buttons, musket balls, cutlery, and pottery fragments of continental soldiers who traveled these woods in Revolutionary times. Events surrounding two Revolutionary War battles took place on land now part of the park. Soldiers involved in the Battle of Fort Montgomery in 1777 and the Battle of Stony Point in 1779 made use of trails around the north and west sides of Bear Mountain and through the hamlet of Queensboro.

Within the natural glory of the park are the reminders of human endeavor in the form of pathways, some used for thousands of years. Many are now known as marked hiking trails for park visitors but long ago were well-traveled routes for commerce, communication, socialization, and revolution, linking the cultures rooted here with each other and with the past.

Rock Shelter. Native American presence in the Hudson Highlands and Ramapo mountains dates back to 10,500 BC. Within Harriman State Park, there are dozens of documented prehistoric sites, including the rock shelter pictured here. Studies by archaeologist Edward Lenik reveal that items unearthed here include a glass bead, clay pipe fragments, buttons, an English coin, and rum bottle fragments. These finds indicate contact with Europeans after 1600. (Coffey collection.)

Log Cabin. Beehives surround an old log cabin tucked in the mountains. Iron mining brought the first settlers to the Highlands and Ramapos in the early 1700s. Iron furnaces required large amounts of wood and charcoal to fuel their constant fires, so woodcutting became an important livelihood. Log cabins provided homes for families who farmed, raised animals, kept bees, and hunted deer and small game.

SMOKEHOUSE. Snow blankets this smokehouse near Baileytown. Mountain residents recall that pigs were slaughtered in November around Election Day. Smoking of hams and bacon quickly followed. Beneath the smokehouse was a fire pit. Warm, dry air from a slow fire was best for curing meat.

BUGGY. A farmer and his two sons pose with their horse and buggy on a park road around 1920. Within the park boundaries, miles of wagon roads connected communities with places of business. Horses, donkeys, and oxen pulled various conveyances through the mountains carrying iron ore, timber, charcoal, and, at times, families.

GREENWOOD FURNACE. Erected in 1811 by James Cunningham, the Greenwood Furnace near Arden, above, supplied cannonballs to Americans during the War of 1812. It was purchased by Robert Parrott, a graduate of West Point and inventor of the Parrott gun, a Civil War cannon. Ore from local mines, some owned by the Parrott family, was hauled to the furnaces, made into pig iron, and transported over the mountains by oxcart to docks along the Hudson for shipment to New York City or the West Point Foundry at Cold Spring.

BARNES MINE. Seven miners stand at the entrance to the Barnes Mine. Farmers often opened mines on their property and worked them with the help of neighbors and relatives. Opened in 1846 by Isaac Barnes, this mine was sold to John Charleston in 1864 and was leased to the Rockland Nickel Company in 1871. It remained in operation until 1884.

BRADLEY MINE. Over 20 abandoned iron mines exist within the boundaries of the park. Here the author surveys the entrance to the Bradley Mine. Opened around 1730, it produced ore until 1874. In the mid-1800s, many more mines were purchased by Robert Parrott, who processed the ore at his Greenwood furnaces near Arden. Numerous iron mines were worked in the Hudson Highlands between 1740 and the 1930s. (Coffey collection.)

Gen. Anthony Wayne. Born in Pennsylvania in 1745, Anthony Wayne (commemorated at left) became a surveyor and state legislator. As colonel of a militia regiment, he fought against the British in Canada. Known for bravery and boldness, Wayne rose to the rank of major general and was chosen by Washington in 1779 to lead 1,300 troops in the assault on Stony Point, an American fort on the Hudson River that had been captured by the British in May 1779. The surprise attack in July 1779 was successful. After a brutal bayonet fight, the Americans recaptured the fort. Wayne received a medal from Congress for his action and continued to distinguish himself throughout the revolution. (Both engravings by Felix Darley.)

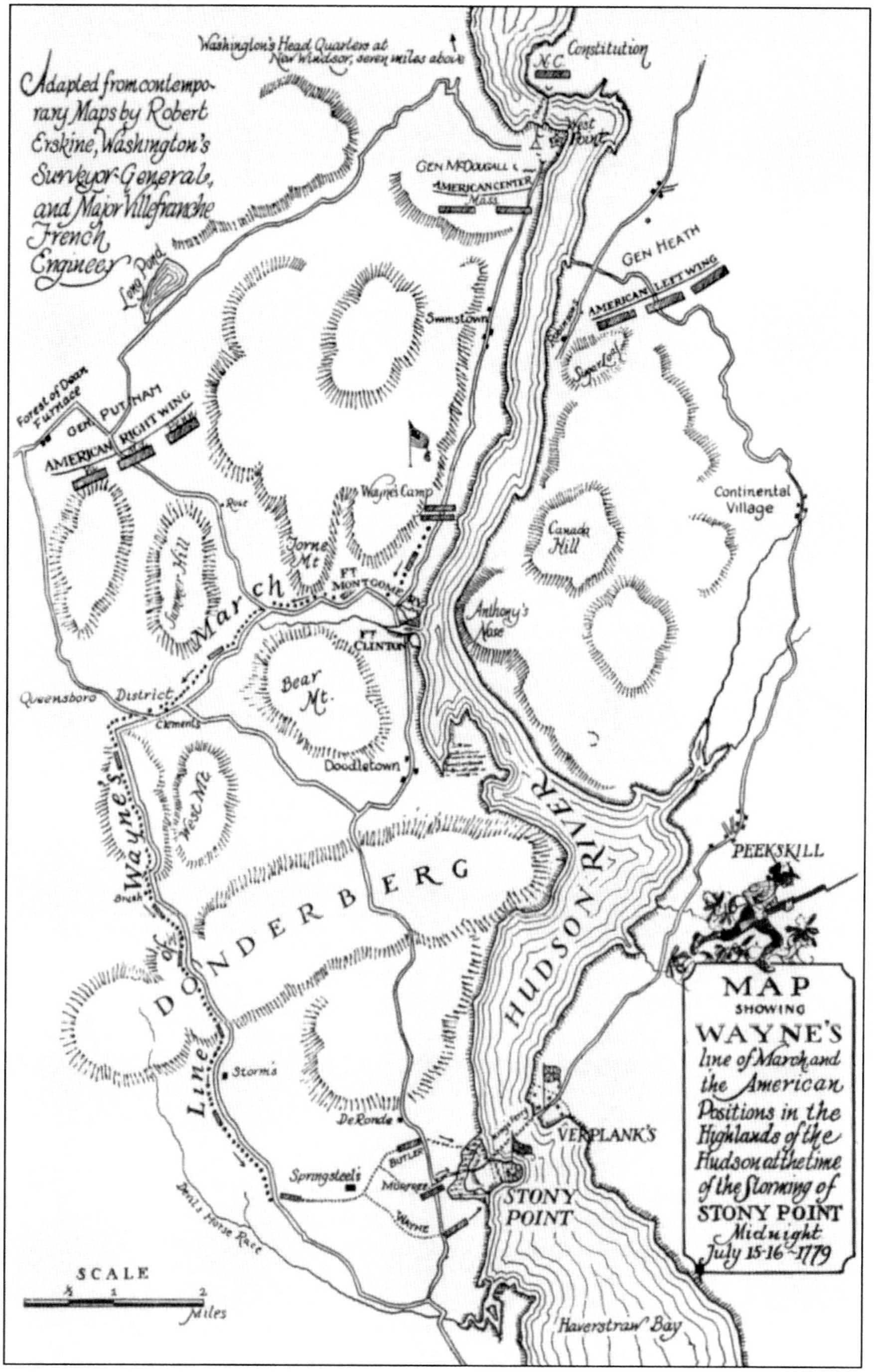

Wayne's March. On July 16, 1779, Wayne prepared a report to his commander, George Washington, describing the defeat of the British at Stony Point. "Our officers and men," he wrote, "behaved like men who are determined to be free." Wayne's infantry had marched from Sandy Beach, near Highland Falls, over "high mountains, through deep morasses, and difficult defiles" of what is now Harriman State Park. This map details the route southwest through Queensboro and then southeast to Stony Point.

Forts Clinton and Montgomery. On October 6, 1777, the British attacked the twin forts, Clinton and Montgomery, on the Hudson River at Popolopen Creek, seen in the painting above. They came north from Caldwell's Landing near Stony Point, to Doodletown where they divided into two columns. One looped around Bear Mountain to Queensboro and proceeded to attack from the rear. The drawing below depicts the march. Despite a gallant defense, the British won, but the delay was costly. It prevented the British from reinforcing their troops further north, leading to an American victory at Saratoga. (Both, artwork by Jack Mead, PIPC Archives.)

Two

Gone but Not Forgotten

During the 19th century, the mountains and valleys of what is now Harriman State Park were home to about 2,200 people. Most of the settlers lived in small hamlets, although many had homes scattered among the hills. Citizens of Queensboro, Pine Meadow, Johnsontown, Sandyfield (also known as Beaver Pond), Baileytown, and Pittsboro engaged in timbering, charcoal production, mining, and farming. They hunted and fished to provide food for their families. Many augmented their income by making baskets known as "bockeys." There were schools, churches, wagon roads, farmhouses, barns, gardens, fields, and orchards. People from the villages gathered for social events like square dances, family celebrations, and prayer.

In 1910, when the Harriman land donation became a park, an additional endowment was added to acquire private homesteads to enlarge the park. Moreover the Palisades Interstate Park Commission was empowered with eminent domain. Essentially it could require homeowners to move. On the one hand the PIPC was committed to preserving as much land as possible to save it from development and returning it to a pristine forest. On the other hand was the heartbreaking reality of families, some of whose roots went back two centuries, forced off their ancestral land. In the 1940s, park police lieutenant James Gazaway shared this refection with his family, "The hardest thing I ever had to do was to remove those people from their land."

Making use of the newly acquired properties, the PIPC converted houses into mess halls or dormitories for campers. Low-lying farms were flooded to make new lakes. Soon overgrown "woods roads" were all that remained of the wide paths originally used to bring out wood for the lumber and charcoal industries. Once bustling with wagons, buggies, horseback riders, and foot traffic, they became hiking trails.

During the construction of the park, certain cemeteries were relocated but some remain, reminding the hiker that once upon a time there were communities here. Many descendants of those named on the burial markers lost their way of life so that the public could enjoy the glory of the woods forever. Today members of the Historical Society of the Palisades Interstate Park Region preserve the memory of the lost hamlets through archives, exhibits, and public events.

SANDYFIELD. Looking west from Jackie Jones Mountain in 1929, the viewer surveyed Sandyfield with its houses, barns, fields, and stonewalls. Founded in 1760, Sandyfield consisted of about 25 homesteads near Beaver Pond. After the creation of the park, commissioners began to acquire private land. Many homeowners resisted through petitions and legal battles, but this only delayed the inevitable. The last residents of Sandyfield left in 1942. The area was transformed into Lake Welch.

ISAIAH JONES'S STORE. Sandyfield was situated on a well-travelled road stretching from Stony Point to Central Valley. In the 1930s, Isaiah Jones operated a grocery store here. It was a favorite gathering place for local men who crowded around the stove sharing news. Jones added a gas station as the Model T arrived in the mountains. The building was shared with the Haverstraw Police Department. The property was sold to the park in 1941.

Sandyfield Schoolhouse. Looking down along the Haverstraw Turnpike, Sandyfield's one-room schoolhouse is seen at left with its flag flying proudly. The dark posts, also at left, mark Odell Lane. Beyond it in the distance is the home of Lyman Prittiman Odell, one of the homesteads flooded by the lake. Rev. Austin Conklin Jr., who documented the life in the hamlets that would soon disappear, took the photograph.

Sarah and Lyman Odell. Sarah Gresh Odell and her husband, Lyman Prittiman Odell, are enjoying a quiet moment on the porch of their Sandyfield home in 1917. Lyman was a lifelong resident of Sandyfield, and his children settled there as well. (Schaper collection.)

CHARLESTON FAMILY. The Charleston family gathered on the porch of their Sandyfield home in 1903. From left to right are Jerome, Olive, Russell, and Phoebe holding Gladys. Typical of the resourceful mountain residents, Jerome was a skilled blacksmith, woodcutter, farmer, miner, as well as storekeeper and deputy sheriff. Phoebe farmed, gardened, cooked, canned, sewed, tended animals, and raised the children. Both parents made baskets and ladles for sale.

ODELL FAMILY. The family of Clarence Prittiman Odell (above, left) posed for this photograph around 1915 on the porch of their handsome house in Sandyfield. With him are his children, Dorothy, Lyman, and Clarence, and his wife, Mathilda. Odell attended the New York School of Design and became a prominent interior decorator. Among his clients were songwriter Irving Berlin and actor Burgess Meredith. The house, with its apple orchard and vineyard, stood behind the Sandyfield School. (Schaper collection.)

Albert Baisley (1868–1948). Pictured here around 1928, Albert Baisley was a resident of Sandyfield. Baisley was one of the area residents who resisted the PIPC acquisition of their land. His house and the surrounding farm were sold to the park in 1942. The property was later covered by Lake Welch.

Rose Cabin. Outdoorsman William Howell photographed John Rose, at left, his wife, Mary, and six of their children beside their cabin in 1910. He described the family as, "American to the core, and of many generations standing." A longtime observer of the mountain people, Howell knew that their way of life was dying out. "The coming of the state parks," he wrote, "means the passing of the old ways." (Photograph by William Howell, PIPC Archives.)

JOSEPH CONKLIN HOMESTEAD. The prosperous homestead of Joseph W. Conklin on Little Long Pond is seen in this photograph taken in spring 1939. With its root cellar, old house, outhouse, chicken coop, and garage, it was representative of many homesteads in the Ramapo Mountains and the Highlands.

CONKLIN HOME. On the afternoon of May 3, 1914, family members sat in front of the Timothy Conklin home near Johnsontown. From left to right are (seated) Mrs. Albert Waldron, her baby boy, "Aunt Mary" Waldron, and Mary Waldron; (standing) Albert Mathers and Tunison Waldron. The Waldrons owned two family farms that were sold to the park in 1917. They were located near the current site of the Lake Sebago Cabins.

JOHNSONTOWN STORE. Timothy Conklin's store in Johnsontown is pictured here around 1929. James Johnson originally settled Johnsontown in the mid-1700s. He cut lumber for the shipbuilding industry, providing tall trees for the masts of ships. Later the area became a thriving farm community.

JONES HOMESTEAD. The homestead of Luther and Lucinda Jones overlooked the waters of Lake Sebago in 1951. Although the rustic cabins of early mountain residents were in evidence, this large frame house, big barn, and outbuildings were more typical of the farms throughout the hills. The Joneses reluctantly left when the new Sebago Beach opened in 1952.

JOHNSONTOWN SCHOOL. The Johnsontown School, pictured here in 1933, was part of District No. 5 of the Towns of Haverstraw and Tuxedo. Aside from their studies, students had to draw water for the school from a nearby spring. The building was originally constructed as the Johnsontown Church around 1871. It was sold to the park in 1947.

BAILEYTOWN SCHOOL. There were 29 students that sat for their class photograph at Baileytown School around 1918. The area around Upper Twin Lake was home to many members of the Bailey family.

Samuel Bailey Jr. (1880-1950). Born in Baileytown, Samuel Bailey Jr. began his working life as a woodcutter for E. H. Harriman. He cleared the cable railway path, the road to the mansion, and several bridle paths. His son recalls him leaving the house each day to walk over the mountain to work, axe in one hand and lunch pail in the other. Harriman later recommended Bailey for a job with the PIPC where he became the foreman and sawmill operator at the park commission's own sawmill at Twin Lakes. Starting in 1924, the park acquired Baileytown properties. Irving Bailey, the last surviving resident, died in 1947. His stone house is pictured below. It was located southeast of Upper Twin Lake on the camp road to Arden.

St. John's Church. Built as a memorial to her husband, St. John's Church in the Wilderness was funded by New York City resident Margaret Zimmerman. It is an Episcopal church and, until 1918, housed a school for orphaned city boys and sons of local mountain families. Services continue to be held every Sunday. The Palm Sunday hiker's service is a special annual event.

Johnsontown Methodist Church. Built in 1872, the Johnsontown Methodist Church stood on the current Lake Welch drive. The park razed it in 1950. At that time, the minister was Rev. Austin Conklin. James Johnson founded Johnsontown around 1750. He supported himself and his family by cutting trees for ship masts.

Brooks House (1918). The abandoned home of Harvey Brooks sits beside the barn and orchard that once provided sustenance for his family. Purchased by the park around 1918, it was converted into Camp Quannacut. The house was at Queensboro, a crossroads community at the intersection of north-south and east-west routes. Today the site is the junction of Long Mountain Parkway (Route 6), Seven Lakes Drive, and the Palisades Interstate Parkway.

Odell Cabin (c. 1925). This charming cabin near Queensboro Lake was built by Rutledge Irving Odell. Odell, a laborer since childhood, insisted that his son, Walter, attend college. Walter graduated from Princeton in 1906 and served in France during World War I. Rutledge intended this as a father-son hunting lodge but died before his boy returned from the war. It was acquired by the park commission around 1920 and became part of a camp.

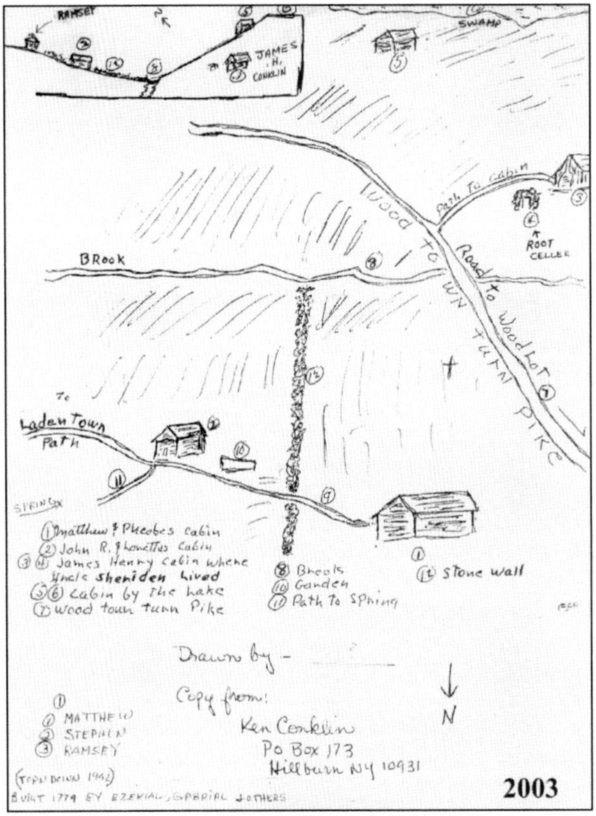

CONKLIN MAP. This map of the Pine Meadow area was hand drawn by Ken Conklin, a descendant of former residents of the current parkland. In the upper left-hand corner of the map is the site of the Ramsey Conklin cabin seen below.

CONKLIN CABIN. Ramsey Conklin was living alone at age 78 in this 200-year-old cabin at Pine Meadow when he had to leave in 1935. His property, including the family cemetery, was being flooded to create Pine Meadow Lake. To comfort him, sympathetic park workers carried fieldstones to erect a marker that would rise above the level of the lake. Over time the memorial disappeared, but it has recently been restored.

Three

The Harrimans

In his youth Edward Harriman spent a summer away from the flat expanse of his boyhood home in Hempstead, Long Island, and worked in the Ramapo Mountains with the family of his friend Richard Parrott, owners of the Greenwood Furnace and nearby mines. It was here that he developed a lifelong love for the mountains, lakes, and forest.

Ambitious and intelligent, Harriman worked his way up from messenger to broker at the New York Stock Exchange. In 1879, he married Mary Williamson. By 1901, he was a powerful board member of three major railroads—the Illinois Central, the Union Pacific, and the Southern Pacific. In 1885, the Parrott estate was for sale so he bought it at auction to prevent its exploitation by lumber companies. Dairy farming continued, but timbering was stopped. Harriman was intent on conservation and reforestation. Soon he acquired adjacent lands creating an estate of almost 30 square miles, which he called Arden.

In March 1909, Harriman learned of the plan to relocate Sing Sing Prison to Bear Mountain. Alarmed at the thought of a prison on his eastern boundary, he worked out a plan with George W. Perkins Sr., president of the Palisades Interstate Park Commission (PIPC), to give 19 square miles of his property and $1 million to acquire additional property between his land and the Hudson River for the creation of parkland. Harriman feared not only the prison, but the encroachment of the city with people crowded "too close for the health of mind and body."

E. H. Harriman died in September 1909, but Mary respected her husband's commitment with several conditions. She insisted that the state raise $1.5 million by private subscription as well as provide matching funds for road building and park development. Within one year, the conditions were met and the deal was finalized at a ceremony on Bear Mountain. Through the years, the Harrimans continued their relationship with the park commission. Their son, Averell, served as commissioner and was an advocate for the park as governor of New York. The Harriman family maintains an estate adjacent to the park and supports the work of the commission to this day.

E. H. Harriman (1848–1909). Assisted by his coachman, Edward Harriman, in gentlemanly attire, arrives at his New York City destination around 1901. As a young teenager, Harriman worked as an errand boy on Wall Street. Through hard work, determination, and unusual business acumen, he rose to be a member of the New York Stock Exchange by age 22. At 50, he was the director of the Union Pacific Railroad, president of the Southern Pacific Railroad, and a board member of several other rail lines. Below is his "special train" that ran on the Erie Railroad, a line which took him to the station in Arden, New York. From there it was a 3-mile carriage ride to his home. (Both, courtesy of Library of Congress.)

Mary Averell Harriman (1852–1932). At the age of 31, E. H. Harriman married Mary Williamson Averell, the daughter of William Averell, president of the Ogdensburg and Lake Champlain Railroad Company in upstate New York. After their marriage, Mary's father offered E. H. a seat on the board of the railroad, which led to his lifelong leadership in the rail industry. The Harrimans had five children: Mary, Henry Neilson, Cornelia, William Averell, and Edward Roland. (Courtesy of Library of Congress.)

Mary and Edward Harriman. Mary Harriman shared her husband's concern over the construction of Sing Sing Prison in neighboring Bear Mountain After Edward's death in 1909, she chose to honor his commitment to offer the State of New York 10,000 acres of land for a state park and $1 million in cash as an endowment to manage it, if they would cease work on the prison and contribute to purchasing more land. On October 29, 1910, the Harrimans presented 10,000 acres of land and $1 million to the PIPC.

HARRIMAN HOME (1905). Arden House, seen here under construction, sits atop a ridge overlooking the Ramapo River valley. Architects Carrere and Hastings designed the magnificent mansion. To bring materials to the site, the 300 workmen used a 1,000-foot cable railway, at far right, up the side of the mountain. The Harriman family later used it until an automobile road replaced it. (Courtesy Library of Congress.)

SING SING. In 1908, New York State began relocation of Sing Sing Prison from Ossining to Bear Mountain. This enclosure housed prisoners who had begun construction. Not wanting to have a prison in the "backyard" and legitimate concern for the protection of scenery caused a public outcry. After the Harriman family donated 10,000 acres of adjacent land and $1 million for creation of a park, the planned prison was abandoned. The playfield at Bear Mountain State Park occupies this area today.

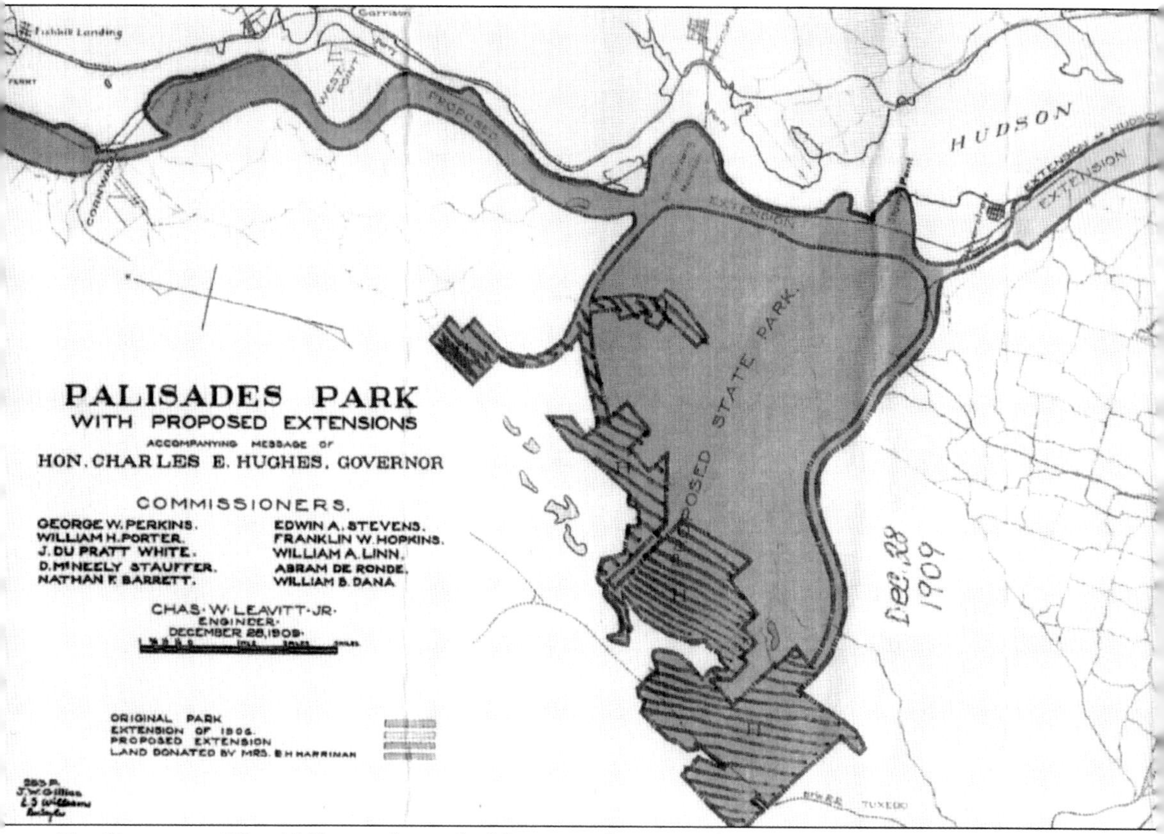

THE PROPOSAL. This 1909 map shows the Harriman donation of 10,000 acres in a striped pattern and the boundaries of the proposed state park. The understanding was that the State of New York would contribute the land to the north and west (Bear Mountain area) and gradually acquire the private land in between. This was not the first time E. H. Harriman had been involved with park creation. He was a friend and ally of naturalist John Muir, supporting his efforts to establish national parks. Over the years the Harriman family has made additional land donations to enlarge and improve Harriman State Park. (Stalter collection.)

The Gift. In September 1910, a ceremony took place on top of Bear Mountain. Onlookers seated downhill observed as E. H. Harriman's eldest son, 19-year-old Averell Harriman, presented the deed for 10,000 acres and a check for $1 million to the State of New York. Receiving the documents, George Perkins responded, "By this act you have conveyed a fortune and a domain." Thus began the creation of Bear Mountain and Harriman State Parks.

Dedication. Mary Harriman, seated third from left in the front row, remained involved to some degree with the Palisades Interstate Park Commission for the remainder of her life. She is pictured here at Bear Mountain. In 1929, she received the Pugsley Gold Medal, an award honoring champions of parks and conservation. The Harriman family continues its support of the park commission.

Four

Park Creation

Harriman, nine times larger than its sister park, Bear Mountain, contains 46,613 acres, extending about 15 miles from north to south and 5 miles from east to west. The development of both parks began immediately after the land acquisition in 1910. The PIPC's mission was to make parks accessible and usable for the public. They were the product of the administrative genius of park commission president George W. Perkins and the engineering mastery of Maj. William A. Welch.

In 1912, Welch was hired by Perkins to be general manager and chief landscape engineer of the Palisades Interstate Park Commission. Welch's accomplishments were numerous. He improved and extended a road to connect the two parks. Later named Seven Lakes Drive, it opened in 1915. Local bridges were constructed to improve accessibility to the parks. Other projects included additional scenic roads, trails, shelters, dams, beaches, playgrounds, pavilions, water and sanitation systems, and dozens of camps. Mountains denuded by overcutting were reforested. Welch had the park legally declared a fish and game preserve, thereby protecting animal habitats, which led to a resurgence of native fauna. As the private automobile became the transportation mode of choice, facilities for motor camping were built. Early on, Welch denied requests to build rental cabins fearing resort development. Instead he championed public access, mindful of a goal to operate the park without commercial gain.

Lakes were the heart of the park. By 1929, around 3,000 acres of water had been added by damming swamps and enlarging existing bodies of water. This work continued during the Depression years when the park received an infusion of labor from the Works Progress Administration (WPA) and the Civilian Conservation Corps (CCC). The young men built dams, roads, and ski trails and constructed 10 more lakes.

Projects like these had never been done on such a scale in public parkland. Because of his visionary leadership at Harriman and Bear Mountain State Parks, Welch became an advisor to the National Park System and to other states and countries as far away as New Zealand, influencing the way parks are created and managed to this day.

George W. Perkins Sr. (1862–1920). George Walbridge Perkins Sr. rose from a modest background to become a powerful businessman and conservationist. Business interests led to a meeting with Gov. Theodore Roosevelt in 1900. Impressed by Perkins, Roosevelt invited him to serve as president of the newly formed Palisades Interstate Park Commission. During his 20-year tenure, Perkins was the guiding force in developing the Palisades Park system, negotiating land purchases, raising funds, and overseeing services.

Major Welch. An army veteran and civil engineer with experience in Alaska and South America, Welch served the PIPC as general manager and chief landscape engineer for 40 years, planning and overseeing the infrastructure to support millions of visitors. Major Welch's creative innovations were termed "revolutionary and evolutionary." His unprecedented accomplishments gained national attention, and he became an advisor to the National Park System and park systems worldwide.

ENGINEERING CAMP. These tents housed a crew of engineers and workers who were busy with two projects at Bockey Swamp in the early 1920s. Major Welch planned a lake in the area that would eventually be called Silvermine Lake. Meanwhile a highway to that lake was being surveyed to enter the park at Sloatsburg and connect to the Seven Lakes Drive.

REFORESTATION. Trucks carried spruce trees through the park in March 1928. Replanting the bare hills was an important project. The forests had been clear-cut multiple times for lumber, charcoal, and firewood for the local brickyards. The commission planted pine, hemlock, walnuts, butternuts, sunflowers, laurel, and hollyhocks. Some plantings were intended as food and cover for game. Within 20 years, the denuded hills were alive with trees, shrubs, flowering plants, and ferns.

LUMBER. A truck pulling four loads of wood makes its way through Harriman State Park around 1918. The clearing of areas for camps and trails, along with the removal of diseased chestnut trees dying from blight, generated a significant amount of timber that was transported to sawmills in the park. The lumber was used for park and camp buildings, docks, benches, and other projects.

SAWMILL (1920). As the park was groomed and reforested, felled trees were used in construction projects. Above, the Lower Twin Lake sawmill is seen in operation. Below, wagons are loaded with lumber to be hauled to locations around the park. Other sawmills existed in Johnsontown and Car Pond. Laborers were hired from hamlets within the park and the surrounding communities.

POPOLOPEN DRIVE. Pictured above, a steam shovel clears rocky debris for the creation of Popolopen Drive. This road was built around the north side of Bear Mountain to connect the western approach to the Bear Mountain Bridge with the Seven Lakes Drive at Queensboro. Below, the first strip of concrete is laid on April 21, 1925. This road made access easier to both Bear Mountain and Harriman Parks. It became part of the Palisades Interstate Parkway.

QUEENSBORO DAM. Construction of the Queensboro Dam is pictured here. After the opening of the park in 1910, the popularity of water sports was immediately evident. Artificial bodies of water to support the numerous camps were created after 1913 by enlarging existing lakes or damming swamps to convert them into lakes. During the first 15 years, 12 new lakes were created. A total of 18 were envisioned.

COHASSET. The massive dam built to create Lake Cohasset in the Arden Valley is clearly seen here. Cohasset means "place of pines." There were actually two man-made sister lakes known as Upper and Lower Cohasset. The lower lake was completed in 1919, and the upper lake was finished in 1922.

Seven Lakes Drive. The *Palisades Interstate Park Commission Annual Report 1915* included this description of the new road. "The drive is 11 miles long, carefully located and graded. The curves are all light and provided with good views." Soon thousands of cars would be driving over it annually, necessitating motorcycle police to regulate traffic and curtail speed.

Queensboro Motor Camp. At the urging of Major Welch, the PIPC created motor camps alongside the scenic park roads to accommodate daytime or overnight visitors. This shady grove was the Queensboro Motor Camp site. It had six outdoor ovens, three rugged stone fireplaces, two latrines, a drinking water system, and concrete tables. Other motor camps were built at Bockey Swamp near Silvermine Lake, and Youman's Meadow, along the Seven Lakes Drive.

Campsite. Each motor campsite had a picnic table and ample parking room. The *Palisades Interstate Park Commission Annual Report 1922* noted the large increase in "the number of automobilists who came with their basket lunches for picnics away from the more congested areas." A campsite could be occupied for 24 hours without a permit. Signs reminded visitors, "Be careful with fires. Clean up before you leave."

Outing. "Campfire" marshmallows and "Drake's" cakes are among the goodies on this picnic table. This scene in 1948 is typical of the simple pleasures of an outing in the country. The photograph answers the rhetorical question posed in the *Palisades Interstate Park Commission Annual Report 1922*: "What can be more delightful, beneficial, or economical to a family or group of friends than a day spent together in the open?"

Summit Lake House. Although most camps were built from scratch, existing structures were often converted into camp buildings. Construction workers are seen here remodeling a guesthouse into a mess hall. This was the Summit Lake House, a three-story hotel owned by Elisha Stockbridge. Edward Harriman purchased the hotel on 35 acres in 1905. It was used as a camp until 1930.

Quannacut. The stately Harvey Brooks House at Queensboro was converted into a mess and recreation hall in 1919. Wide verandas and a protected eating area were added. Named Camp Quannacut, it served as both a summer and winter camp.

House to Hall. The house and barn that belonged to the Weygant family are seen above as they undergo conversion into camp facilities. Below, the Lewis house has been fitted with a temporary canvas cover to create a mess hall. Camp O.L.L. from the Church of Our Lady of Lourdes used the latter facility from 1920 to 1921. The houses were near Upper Twin Lake.

TENTS. Large tent platforms supported heavy canvas canopies with adjustable sides to take advantage of good weather. Living quarters were designed for maximum exposure to fresh air. These tents housed young boys at Lake Stahahe around 1918.

CAMP CREATION. With its mission to bring city children into the wilderness, the creation of camps was a major PIPC initiative. They were located near lakefronts for easy accessibility to swimming and boating facilities. Camp Watchung at Upper Twin Lake is an example.

SLEEPING CABINS. This view of Camp Te Ata at Lower Twin Lake shows the construction of 18-foot-by-18-foot sleeping cabins with overhanging roofs, open to the fresh air. A combination of tents and cabins were utilized at many camps. Camp Te Ata was located along Route 6.

COMMUNITY BUILDING. This hall at Tiorati was a 1920s WPA project designed by Welch after plans by architect Charles Leavitt, employed by the Rockefeller family. Workers in this federal program commuted from Manhattan and were bussed to their work site. Park foreman Samuel Bailey recalled that the first crew, unfamiliar with the rugged terrain, arrived in patent leather shoes. Soon however, they were trained, outfitted, and made notable contributions to the park.

Civilian Conservation Corps. Laborers from the Civilian Conservation Corps (CCC) are seen above clearing a swamp. During the Great Depression, the federal government put unemployed men to work on projects for the public good. The first of the park's CCC camps was built in 1933 at Beechy Bottom near the present-day Anthony Wayne Recreation area. The camps consisted of wooden barracks, a mess hall, officers club, quarters, and storage buildings. By 1934, about 2,000 men were at work clearing swamps and building dams, sewage and water systems, fire roads, and 10 lakes, including Pine Meadow, Welch, Silvermine, Skannatati, and Skenonto. Below, Pine Meadow Dam is shown under construction as project foremen check the day's progress. It was one of the first CCC projects completed. Their work continued until 1942.

Five

CAMPS

The history of Harriman Park is deeply entwined in camping. Camp units were built around the lakes and then rented to social, charitable, or philanthropic organizations. By 1917, camping had grown so significantly in popularity that the Palisades Interstate Park Commission created a separate department. At its maximum in the 1920s and 1930s, Harriman Park hosted 102 camps operated by about 500 organizations. This was later reduced to the more manageable number of 71. The commission built campsites along the lakes and leased them to organizations for short or long-term use. The Boy Scouts started camping in Harriman as early as 1913, being the first to enjoy the surroundings, followed quickly by Girl Scouts, Campfire Girls, and the YWCA. The commission stressed the need to expose the urban poor to the wilderness to improve their health and make them better citizens. The diverse list of organizations that operated camps grew to include the Association for Improving the Condition of the Poor, the Hebrew Orphan Asylum, the Boy's Club, the Temporary Relief Administration, the New York Association for the Blind, the Brooklyn Home for Destitute Children, and various religious organizations and settlement houses. Early camps were not only for children. Some were for mothers and babies, hiking clubs, families, or vacationing adult factory workers. During the Depression, Camp TERA, named for its sponsor, the Temporary Relief Administration, welcomed unemployed women. Lake Stahahe became the site of nutrition camps that were sponsored by philanthropic organizations. Summit, Cohasset, and Twin Lakes were reserved for girls' camps. The Kanawauke Lakes area was primarily for Boy Scouts. Lake Tiorati had a mixture of camps.

Facilities had a standardized construction pattern that included a recreation and/or mess hall, a lakeside dock, sleeping and administrative cabins, tent platforms, washhouse, latrines, and several rowboats and canoes. An elaborate infrastructure provided clean, safe water to all the camps. By 1922, the demand for new sites exceeded the funds available to build them so the PIPC allowed organizations to donate money for the cost of constructing a camp for them in exchange for a lease. The New York Life Insurance Company and R. H. Macy thus provided recreation for their employees and their families. Camping continues to be an important part of the park's mission.

First Camp. The history of camping in Harriman State Park dates back to 1913 when the first camp was established on Car Pond, later called Lake Stahahe, for the Boy Scouts of Greater New York. In 1917, the scouts were relocated to a larger and more isolated complex of 17 camps at Kanawauke, a chain of three lakes at the center of the park. The Boy Scout camp brochure touted it as "keen country, wild, big, away from everywhere with inspiring heights." The Boy Scout program included hikes to West Point, iron mines, Bear Mountain, and Island Pond. Pictured above is their general headquarters. Below, the interior of the headquarters pavilion is seen crowded with scouts and scoutmasters. A park policeman is visible at far right. The park police regularly patrolled the camps throughout Harriman and Bear Mountain State Parks. The nighttime shift was known as the "mosquito patrol."

Transportation. In the 1920s, the New York area Boy Scouts travelled to the park by three routes. They could come by rail to the Southfields, New York, station aboard the Erie Railroad, by the West Shore Railroad to the Bear Mountain station, or by boat from New York City to the Bear Mountain dock. From those points, they were bussed to their assigned camps. By 1926, the PIPC owned 45 omnibuses, primarily for transporting campers. Above, a 25-passenger bus, carrying eager young campers, travels the Seven Lakes Drive. Below, two groups of scouts arrive at a Kanawauke camp.

Troop Formation. This well-disciplined troop of Boy Scouts posed for a group photograph on a summer day in 1920. They were attending one of the 17 scout camps around Lower, Middle, and Upper Kanawauke Lakes. By this time, daily attendance exceeded 2,000 boys that were ready to experience outdoor cooking, mapmaking, weather prediction, and finding their way in the woods.

Overnight Camp (c. 1921). Aside from their regular lakeside camps, the Boy Scouts of Greater New York utilized smaller, more remote camps such as this one. Scouts made significant contributions in trail work. They were responsible for the marking of the White Bar Trail, a 35-mile circle around the three Kanawauke Lakes. Five spokes connected back to the center, and along those spokes were small overnight camps called Forest, Leatherstocking, Hawkeye, Pathfinder, Prairie, and Deerslayer.

Camp Director. Ruby Jolliffe, seated at center above, with a group of camp employees, became the director of park camps in 1920, the first female executive hired by the PIPC. A former coordinator of YWCA camps, she was a lively and imposing presence, deeply concerned with discipline, health, programs, nature education, food, sports, morals, and morale. During her 28-year tenure, Jolliffe worked closely with Major Welch and befriended Eleanor Roosevelt, a frequent visitor to the camps. She worked constantly to improve the camping experience. Below, park officials make an inspection by rowboat. Seated third from left is Jolliffe. Park police chief William Gee is fourth, and Major Welch is at the far right. Other passengers are unidentified. Known affectionately as "Jolly," the director often made unannounced visits to the camps during the winter and summer.

Sleeping Shacks. Camps had a standardized building plan that included open-air sleeping cabins, such as these at Summit Lake. They were affectionately referred to as "shacks." The interior view below shows girls making their beds. Hooks and shelves spaced along the wall could hold personal items. Prospective campers in 1919 received a checklist of recommended articles to bring, including extra stockings, a nightshirt, handkerchiefs, floating soap, a tin cup, shoestrings, and a fountain pen.

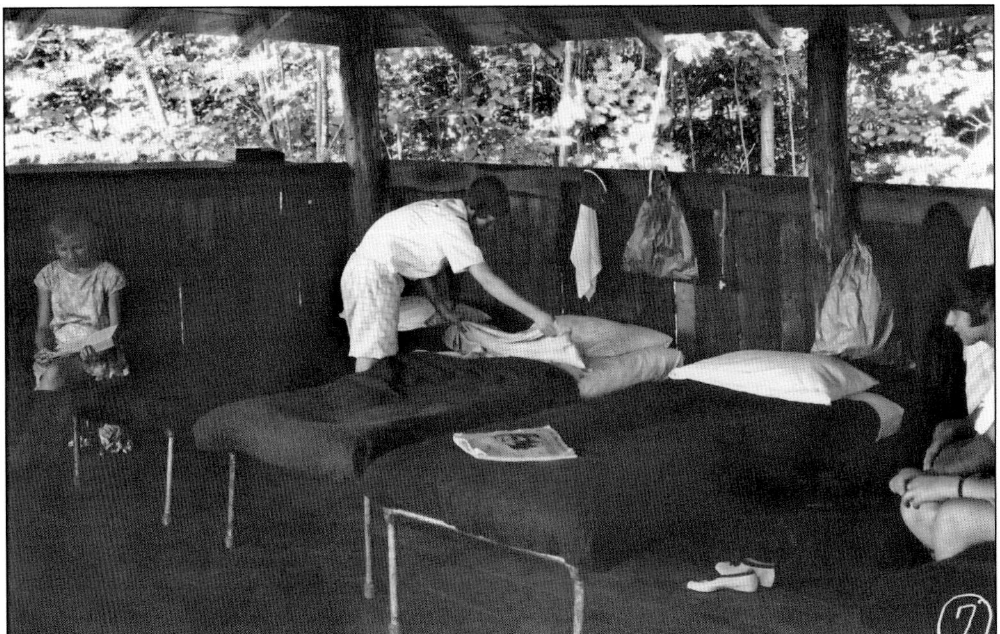

Tenting Tonight. Tent platforms with billowing canvas covers were part of the standard camp construction. The platforms remained year-round, but the tops were removed and stored for the winter. Camp Watchung, above, was managed by the Montclair Girl Scouts. The site was at Upper Twin Lake, a natural lake purchased by the park in 1919. Here tents were arranged in a horseshoe with a common area in the center. Most tents could accommodate eight cots with storage overhead and limited shelving. The sleeping beauties below were at the Girl Scout Camp Manhattan at Lower Twin Lake. Each camp was required to have adequate supervision in the ratio of one counselor to every 10 children.

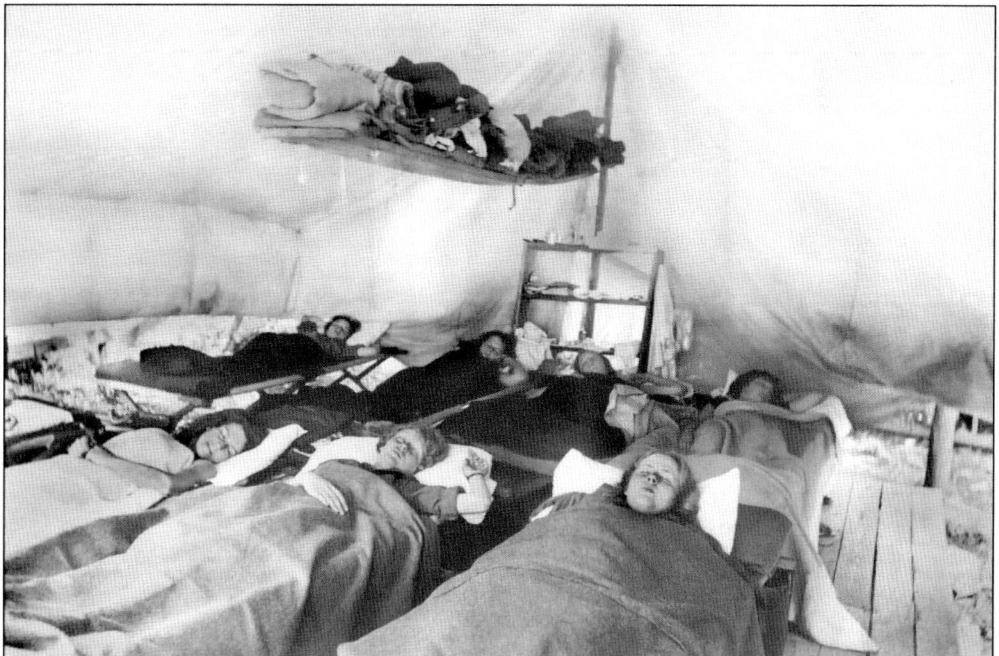

REVEILLE. Camps generally had a military-style organization. Buglers were responsible for reveille, awakening campers to a new morning of activities. At 10:00 p.m. every evening, "Taps" was played after a day full of activities. This bugler was a member of the Young Women's Christian Association (YWCA) at Summit Lake Camp around 1923.

FLAG SALUTE. After reveille, campers assembled for the salute to the flag. This patriotic exercise was standard procedure at the camps. Girl Scouts from Montclair, New Jersey, attending the Camp Watchung were photographed as the flag was raised on a summer morning about 1922.

INSPECTION (1923). Lining up for inspection was another aspect of camp life borrowed from the military. A group of young male campers stand ready and waiting as their faces, teeth, hair, and hands are checked for cleanliness by their counselor. They appear to be recent arrivals at Lake Stahahe.

MORNING EXERCISES (c. 1922). One of the morning rituals at camp was physical exercise. Decked out in their bloomers and blouses, the girls of Camp Quannacut conduct calisthenics at their facility in Queensboro. They are actually on the driveway of the Brooks House, which was purchased by the commission and converted into a mess and recreation hall.

Capers (c. 1948). Chores were another part of the daily routine. The Girl Scouts called them "capers." These involved table setting, washing dishes, tidying the living quarters, scrubbing the washhouse and latrines, sweeping the docks, and picking up litter. Scouts were encouraged to perform their work cheerfully and carefully. These busy young ladies are cleaning up at Camp Wakoda, run by the Newburgh Council of Girls Scouts at Upper Twin Lake.

Cleanup Time (c. 1922). Counselors at the Cedar Lake Camp on Lake Tiorati, above, observe as their charges make a final check of the "hospital corners" on their beds and straighten their blankets. Typically an inspection would follow and points would be awarded for cleanliness and order.

Sanitary Facilities. Health and hygiene were promoted at all the camps. Well-maintained sanitary facilities were required. Above, a group of Boy Scouts uses the washhouse under the watchful eye of their scout leader. Washhouses had six to 10 faucets of running water. Major Welch made it a priority that safe, clean water be provided to the camps via an innovative system of pumps, pipes, and reservoirs. Below is the interior of a chemical latrine. Eventually flush toilets replaced these. The PIPC took pride in a 1925 health report by the commissioner of the Health of the State of New York that stated, "In no similar area in the State are the health conditions better than in the Park."

Double-Decker. The double-decker mess hall debuted around 1925. The upper level served as sleeping quarters for supervisory staff. This fine example was constructed for Camp Osborn at Lower Twin Lake. The Girl Scout Council of Orange, New Jersey, ran the camp.

Social Center. The young ladies of Camp Yorkville on Lake Tiorati called their mess hall a "social center." Here several campers socialize on the rustic staircase. The average stay at camp was two weeks.

Mess Halls. At first, the mess halls were built to serve double duty as recreation halls. Above is the Camp Manhattan mess hall at Lower Twin Lake in 1922. A Girl Scout stands by the stone fireplace. Space has been cleared for a game or activity. A piano is visible at right. Below, a group of boys from Grace Camp at Lake Stahahe utilized their hall for singing practice around 1930. Timber cleared during the construction of dams and lakes was used for the camp buildings along with lumber felled by the chestnut blight.

Cooks. Standing by tables neatly set with china, cooks and camp leaders awaited hungry campers in the mess hall of Cedar Lake Camp around 1922. The Young Men's and Young Women's Hebrew Associations of New Jersey operated the camp. Cedar Lake Camp was on Lake Tiorati.

Mess Tent. Boys are waiting on their lunch in a mess tent set up near the lake in 1925 at another Tiorati location, Camp Stevenson.

Dish Duty. Adult camp leaders pitched in to wash and dry the dishes at the Twin Lakes mess hall in 1920. Camps recruited their own leaders and counselors. The PIPC provided police protection and medical supervision.

Lunch Time (c. 1924). Seated on sturdy benches, these girls are ready to enjoy a hearty lunch. The open-air mess hall took full advantage of the splendid scenery. Although some groups did their own cooking, the majority of the meals were cooked at the Bear Mountain Inn and delivered to the camps.

Waterfront (1943). A typical waterfront structure included a dock, boat storage, a diving board, an offshore raft (not seen), and a "crib." The crib was an enclosed swimming area with a wooden floor for beginners with a water depth of about 3 feet. All camps had a senior Red Cross lifeguard.

Swimming. Young ladies attending the Paulist camp during the 1920s took full advantage of the swimming facilities for morning and afternoon recreation periods. There were two cribs at this large camp at Summit Lake. The dock facilities of a neighboring camp are seen in the background.

Boat Landing. The boat landing was a good place to relax on a sunny day at Summit Lake in 1922. Judging from the camper at left, this landing was also used for diving practice. Rowboats, made by park employees, were in constant demand as the number of lakes, camps, and day visitors increased.

Swimming Race (c. 1923). Onlookers row by to cheer for their favorites in the girls's swimming races at Upper Twin Lake. As children improved their swimming skills, they were permitted to leave the crib, swim in deeper water, and join in friendly competitions.

DIVERS. Demonstrating their best form, campers prepared to spring from the platform at Summit Lake Camp around 1922. Most camps had a simple, low diving board, but facilities varied somewhat from camp to camp. Diving instruction was offered by organizations that employed a certified teacher on staff. In 1926, Thomas Hirshfield, the National High and Fancy Diving Champion, toured the park giving exhibitions and instruction at camps.

Diving. A counselor sat close by as two girls, right, practiced a stunt on the diving board at Camp Wakoda in 1929. The Newburgh Girl Scout Council at Upper Twin Lake operated the camp from 1924 to 1951. Below, a young man executes a graceful swan dive off a high platform at Camp Ken-a-dee at Lake Stahahe.

STAHAHE MEMORIES. Herbert Schwenke treasured his camp experience his whole life. Seated fifth from left in the second row, he appears in this photograph of fellow campers. Schwenke was a New York City boy who spent summers swimming, diving, and rowing at Camp Pequot. He developed a lifelong love of the area and later moved to the Hudson Highlands, returning often to Lake Stahahe with his family. (McCormick collection.)

CANOE TRIP. Off on a journey by canoe, these young ladies paused to be photographed on Queensboro Lake around 1923. A water safety course was a prerequisite to handling a boat of any kind.

Row, Row, Row. Nine members of the YWCA of New York embarked on a boat outing on Summit Lake around 1921. Park commission employees built the hundreds of rowboats that were provided to the camps.

Oarsmen. Teens from Cedar Lake Camp on Lake Tiorati assembled on the dock for rowing practice, flanked by their instructors. Boating was so popular that the PIPC was hard-pressed to keep up with the demand for boats.

Activities. Away from the water, there were abundant activities for campers. Above, a basketball game is under way at Cedar Lake Camp around 1923. Teams of boys from the Young Men's Hebrew Association (YMHA) of New Jersey await the jump ball. Below, a boxing match is in full swing at Globe Camp at Lake Stahahe. The Association for Improving Conditions of the Poor sponsored these young opponents.

Ball Game. Scouts at Camp Watchung gathered by their tents to relax or watch a game of catch with an oversized rubber ball. These girls came from Montclair, New Jersey, to Upper Twin Lake around 1921. For many children, a stay at camp was their first and only chance to hike in a forest, swim in a lake, climb a mountain, create games, and experience the sights and sounds of nature, day and night.

Tent Scene (c. 1922). Seated on the edge of their tent platform, campers at Summit Lake pose for a photograph. Note their fashionable bloomers and high-heeled boots. In the second row, a young woman prepares to take a photograph with a box camera. The two-story barn of the Summit Lake House can be seen in the background. Purchased by the PIPC in 1919, the lodging was a well-known hotel that they converted into a camp facility.

GONE FISHING. Carefully balanced in her rowboat with her fishing pole in hand, a Camp Kittredge girl proudly displays the largemouth bass she caught in Upper Twin Lake around 1923. Fishing was one of the many new experiences for the inner-city children who came to the Harriman camps.

APPLE PICKING (C. 1922). Young ladies of the YWCA camp at Summit Lake enjoy some late summer apple picking near Stockbridge Mountain. Fruit trees and orchards were often found near old homesteads that were abandoned when the park acquired the land.

ARTS AND CRAFTS. One of the regularly scheduled camp activities was an arts and crafts class. These girls from Camp Kittredge are busily at work making little dolls. Key cases and lanyards were other popular crafts. An integral part of the camping experience, handicrafts encouraged a sense of accomplishment.

RESTING AWHILE. The Young Women's Christian Association (YWCA) operated multiple camps in the 1920s. Several young ladies took a break from their daily schedule at Camp Quannacut to rest for a moment on their flag-draped porch on the Fourth of July. Their camp building was the old Brooks House at Queensboro Lake.

Bull's-Eye. A perennially popular activity, archery was practiced through the decades at the camps. Whether during the 1940s, above, or the 1970s, below, proper technique was demonstrated by a skilled instructor and eager campers tried to master it.

SING-ALONG. Singing was an integral part of the camp experience. Rainy days in the recreation hall and evenings around the campfire were good times for group sing-alongs of songs such as "B-I-N-G-O," "Hail, Hail the Gang's All Here," and "Trail the Eagle." Special camp events featured groups such as the one above from Lake Cohasset. Below, a talented camp counselor accompanies some youngsters on guitar at Lake Tiorati around 1970.

CAMP TERA. Five young ladies are gathered around two seamstresses at Camp TERA on Lake Tiorati in August 1933. Sponsored by Eleanor Roosevelt, the camp provided education and recreation for unemployed women. These girls are wearing clothes they designed and made themselves. Camp TERA was funded by New York's Temporary Relief Administration, one of 90 nationwide "She-She-She" camps analogous to the all-male CCC camps of the Civilian Conservation Corps. (Coffey collection.)

WORKSHOP (1940). The family camp at Lake Kanawauke had science equipment in the old Shenstone garage available to youngsters with supervision. Camps tried to broaden the range of children's experiences and foster self-esteem through the satisfaction of mastering a skill.

Be Prepared. Among the useful skills learned at camp were safety and communication. Pictured at right, an instructor demonstrates the Schaefer Method of artificial respiration to Girl Scouts at Camp Wakoda in 1929. Below, two Camp Watchung scouts are practicing signaling with flags.

Broom Race. Every camp had culminating activities at the end of the session. Often they included competitions or shows. This race using brooms instead of oars was a whimsical boating competition held at Camp Wakoda's water circus in 1929.

Water Pageant. Games and spirit events were organized to promote better intercamp relationships. Lake Tiorati was the scene of an impressive nautical pageant that included elaborately decorated vessels from two Cedar Lake facilities. The YMHA and YWHA sponsored these camps from 1925 to 1928. Currently the PIPC continues this tradition with an annual canoe regatta.

Special Events. Through the years, special events remained an eagerly anticipated part of camp life. Above, an interested audience watches a play at a boy's camp around 1941. Below, two costumed girls from Camp Manitou execute a graceful routine on a balance beam as part of a circus at Twin Lake in 1948.

QUIET TIME. These campers are pictured enjoying some quiet time around the fire in the recreation hall. Possibly it was a rainy day. Some read, sketch, or play checkers.

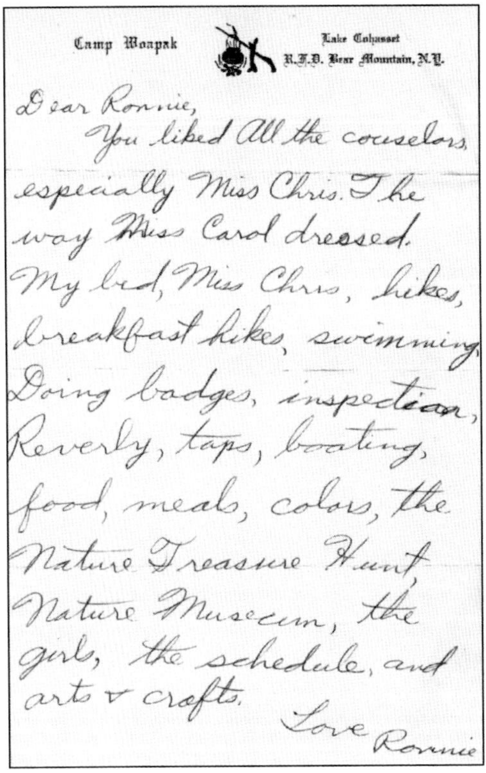

Camp Woapak

Lake Cohasset
R.F.D. Bear Mountain, N.Y.

Dear Ronnie,

You liked All the couselors, especially Miss Chris. The way Miss Carol dressed. My bed, Miss Chris, hikes, breakfast hikes, swimming, Doing badges, inspection, Reverly, taps, boating, food, meals, colors, the Nature Treasure Hunt, Nature Museum, the girls, the schedule, and arts & crafts.

Love Ronnie

LETTER FROM CAMP. Girl Scouts from Paramus, New Jersey, who attended Camp Woapak at Lake Cohasset in 1959 were encouraged to write a letter to themselves on camp stationery summing up their experiences after two weeks. Then each girl mailed her letter home to serve as a memento of her stay at camp. The author discovered hers pasted into an old scrapbook beside a pressed flower and a piece of lanyard. (Coffey collection.)

WORSHIP. Campers were encouraged to attend Sunday services corresponding to their own religions. Facilities were sometimes provided within the park. Above, a tent was utilized as a chapel at Camp Hayes on Lake Tiorati from 1921 to 1924. Below, a Catholic priest prepares to celebrate Mass for campers at Twin Lakes around 1920. Vases of evergreens adorn the rustic altar. Opportunities were also offered for religious services at nearby churches.

Camp Emetowa. Three youngsters, left, take a brief rest from camp activities on the steps of the mess hall at Camp Emetowa at Lake Tiorati. The Negro Fresh Air Committee operated the camp from 1923 to 1931. Below, a group of mother and baby campers assemble for a photograph at Camp Tapawingo at Lake Cohasset. The YWCA of Newburgh ran this camp.

Camp Nylic. Smiling employees of the New York Life Insurance Company assembled for a photograph on Lake Tiorati in 1924. By 1921, the PIPC could no longer afford to meet the demand for camps. The commission began a system of permitting private companies to provide money to build camps and lease the property for a specified time. The New York Life Insurance Company was the first to take advantage of this opportunity. Macy's and Rogers Peet quickly followed.

Masonic Camp. Attendees of the camp administered by the Masonic Club of Haverstraw assembled for a photograph in 1940. They are gathered in front of their picturesque lodge, formerly the home of Joseph Shenstone. It is located at Upper Kanawauke Lake, also known as Little Long Pond, one of the natural lakes in the park. This was a family camp to which members came from many parts of the country.

Franklin D. Roosevelt. On July 27, 1921, Franklin D. Roosevelt (FDR), above left, visited the Boy Scout Camps at Lake Kanawauke as part of his duties as president of the Boy Scout Foundation of Greater New York. Later that day he posed for the camera standing tall, center left, amid a throng of campers and scoutmasters. Evidence suggests that Roosevelt contracted polio during this visit. Two weeks later, on vacation at Campobello, FDR began to exhibit the symptoms of the disease that left his legs permanently paralyzed. These are two of the last official photographs of the future president walking unassisted. Roosevelt staunchly supported the PIPC during his term as governor of New York. "The park idea," he once said, "is essential to American civilization."

SPECIAL VISIT. Eleanor Roosevelt had a particular interest in the Harriman camps. She was committed to broadening the experience of young women. Often she attended ceremonies and participated in activities such as the nature play day in these two photographs. Wearing a white dress, she is seen above, left, on the basketball court. To the right is the camp "orchestra." Below right, she addresses the assembled campers. An eyewitness to one of Roosevelt's visits recalled that she drove up to the camp in a convertible with the top down, her scarf flying in the breeze.

Campfires. One of the favorite wilderness experiences is the campfire at the end of the day. It was a time for storytelling, stunts, skits, ceremonies, pantomimes, solo performances, singing, or reflection. Under the stars, music and laughter echoed across the lakes and through the hills. At the conclusion of the campfire, "Taps" was played or sung to these words: "Day is done. / Gone the sun / from the lake / from the hills / from the sky. / All is well. / Safely rest. / God is nigh."

Six

Recreation

Organized summer camps were by no means the only form of recreation available in the park. An array of diverse activities were centered around the lovely lakes. Public bathing facilities existed at Lakes Tiorati, Sebago, and Kanawuake. Later sandy beaches and snack stands were created at Lakes Tiorati, Welch, and Sebago, making them even more popular as weekend destinations. When not in service delivering supplies to the camps, the service boats were used as tour boats for day visitors. Individual camping was offered at specific locations for $2 per week. Early on, the miles of scenic park roads became known for their stunning beauty. In 1919, a sightseeing bus service from Bear Mountain through Harriman Park was an immediate success. Automobiles, motorcycles, and bicycles utilized Seven Lakes Drive, Tiorati Brook Road, Arden Valley Road, Popolopen Drive, Long Mountain Road (Route 293), and Stony Brook Road. For Sunday drivers, these were a destination unto themselves.

Starting in 1923, three facilities were outfitted for winter occupation by groups. They were provided with electricity and fuel. Cold weather enthusiasts enjoyed tobogganing, ice skating, sledding, and ice fishing. In 1936, the Silvermine area was developed for downhill skiing. Meanwhile cross-country skiing grew steadily in popularity. Harriman's backcountry trails and old woods roads were perfect for this sport. Indoor enjoyment was available as well. The legendary roller-skating rink at Kanawuake drew skaters from Orange and Rockland Counties who still remember the fun. Two years after the rink burned down in 1952, a second rink was built at Lake Sebago.

With the construction of the Palisades Interstate Parkway, the continuous scenic highway from the George Washington Bridge to Bear Mountain and Harriman State Parks was complete. With it came the development of the site known as Anthony Wayne Recreation Area. Three inviting pools attracted families throughout the summer. Although the pools no longer exist, the expansive venue with its ample parking lot remains ideal for special events such as car shows, the county fair, music performances, and ethnic festivals.

WINTER (c. 1928). Pictured above, a party of vacationers waits aboard a park bus for transportation from the Bear Mountain Railroad Station to Camp Quannacut. Located at Queensboro near the present-day Long Mountain Circle, Camp Quannacut was the first winter campsite put in use by the PIPC. Below, a group of Campfire Girls of Greater New York prepares to enjoy some skating and snowshoeing with camps director Ruby Jolliffe, at right. By 1928, there were several winter camps. The girls pictured here boarded at Camp Tulualac at Upper Lake Cohasset.

Campfire Girls. Snowballs in hand, a group of Campfire Girls at Lake Cohasset posed on an old wooden cart. Winter camping began almost as soon as summer camps closed and lasted until the end of March.

Quannacut. By 1924, winter camping was in its third season. The largest was Camp Quannacut in the Queensboro Valley. The PIPC operated it for mixed groups numbering up to 35 people under "proper chaperonage." Cabin rentals started at $20 and included bus transportation for campers from the local train station. A caretaker helped with cooking and cleaning. Toboggans, snowshoes, and skis could be rented. Accompanying these campers was Dr. Benjamin Hyde, the park naturalist, standing eighth from left.

Tobogganing (c. 1923). Toboggan runs were a feature at Camp Quannacut at Queensboro Lake, above, and at Camp Thendara at Lake Tiorati, below. The PIPC was delighted at the response to winter recreation. The *Palisades Interstate Park Commission Annual Report 1923* noted that the young, city people were "fast becoming educated to appreciate the joys of a weekend in the country with various winter sports offered."

CAMPFIRE TONIGHT. Above, a fallen novice skater gets a little help from her friends to the amusement of three onlookers. These girls stayed at Camp Talualac at Upper Cohasset Lake in 1928. The Campfire Girls operated it from 1928 to 1941. Below, some of the campers brave the cold to gather wood, anticipating an evening of warmth and companionship around the fire.

ICE FUN. The frozen expanse of Lake Tiorati was perfect for skating and sledding on this winter day in 1934. Young ladies from Camp TERA took full advantage of the smooth ice. Camp TERA was operated under the auspices of the Temporary Emergency Relief Administration, a federal agency organized during the Great Depression.

Cross-Country Skiing. Equipment in hand, cross-country skiers took a break at a mountaintop trail shelter. The center gentleman, seated, wears the sweater of the Bear Mountain Sports Association. This society sponsored competitions year-round in both parks, including meets for speed skating, figure skating, and swimming.

Camp Thendara. As demand grew, winter camping was conducted at Lakes Kanawauke, Tiorati, Stahahe, Upper Twin, and Upper Cohasset. This photograph shows members of the Appalachian Mountain Club at Camp Thendara on Lake Tiorati around 1925. The club is a hiking organization whose dedicated members built, marked, and maintained trails in the park. Members continue to support the commission doing volunteer trail work.

Silvermine Ski Area. In 1936, a ski slope was created at Lake Menomine, later called Silvermine Lake. The area took its name from the legendary existence of a mysterious silver mine apparently known only to certain Spaniards who visited the area in the 1700s. In 1942, a second hill was developed to accommodate the growing numbers of downhill skiers.

Equipment Shed. Georgia "Sissy" Wallace, in sunglasses, approaches her friend Lucille Neibhur headed for the rope tow in 1955. The equipment shed is visible in the background. Skis could be rented for a nominal fee. (Wallace collection.)

T-Bar. On a clear, crisp day in December 1963, skiers enjoyed a ride to the top of the mountain on a T-bar. By the 1960s, there were two T-bar lifts and a rope tow.

Night Skiing. Sparkling under the lights, the packed snow was inviting to skiers who took advantage of the night hours at Silvermine. The slope was open until 1986.

Ice Fishing. As soon as the ice was thick enough, fishermen were, and still are, a common sight on the Harriman lakes. Warmly dressed, they head out to test their endurance and patience at a favorite spot in the frozen wilderness.

Skating Rink. Kanawauke Skating Rink was the place to be in the 1940s and early 1950s. Resting between dances, Kathleen Cameron, Kathy Jobson, Evva Hevion, Dede Schassler, Eleanor Schmalsteg, and Carol Sailor lent support to their friend Gene Fox. Every summer, teens from Stony Point and other nearby towns arrived for the morning, afternoon, or evening sessions. (Aguanno collection.)

Dance Floor. Benches surrounded the vast floor of the Kanawauke rink for onlookers or tired patrons. Graceful skaters swayed to recorded organ music of waltzes, two-steps, and special dances while guards, skating backwards, maintained order.

Rink Fire. In May 1952, a fire broke out at the rink. The structure burned quickly due to its wood composition and because of chemicals used to preserve the rink from weather and insects. Only the stonework remained. Mindful of the good times, friendships, and happy evenings spent there, many loyal patrons visited the site immediately after the fire to retrieve mementos, such as skate keys, buried beneath the ashes.

Tour Boats. Transporting a party of adventurous ladies, a weekend tour boat crosses Upper Lake Kanawauke around 1920. These large, sturdy craft were used during the week for food delivery to camps. On Saturdays and Sundays, they were used for public tours.

Lake Welch Beach. With its vast sandy beach and wide promenade, Lake Welch Beach was an instant success from the moment of its opening on June 15, 1962. It remains popular with swimmers, boaters, sunseekers, and picnickers. The lake is named for Maj. William A. Welch, general manager and chief landscape engineer of the PIPC from 1912 to 1940.

Picnickers. Three well-dressed motorists stopped along the unpaved road to Cedar Pond in 1911. They had been invited by hiker and nature-lover William Thompson Howell, who snapped their picture. Soon afterward they proceeded to his camp near the current site of Lake Tiorati. Howell, an avid outdoorsman, often entertained guests at campsites in the Hudson Highlands. (Photograph by William Howell.)

Mustang Rally. The driver of this gleaming Ford Mustang arrived at Anthony Wayne Recreation Area in June 1969. The expansive parking lot was the site of the PIPC's annual Mustang rally. These car enthusiasts registered for a pleasant day of socializing with other automobile fans and the possibility of a trophy for an exceptional vehicle.

Anthony Wayne. Anthony Wayne Recreation Area had three separate pools—one for swimming, a deeper pool for diving, and a shallow children's pool. Above, divers line up for a chance to jackknife into the diving pool while others enjoy the sunny June day in 1957. Below, the swimming pool was jammed with Fourth of July bathers in 1961.

Recreation Area. The 35-acre playground named for Revolutionary War hero Anthony Wayne opened in 1955. It was created as part of the Palisades Interstate Parkway construction project. This aerial view attests to its popularity. Amenities included multiple swimming pools, bathhouses, playfields, and a substantial parking lot.

Music Festival. In 1959, the Empire State Music Festival was held at Anthony Wayne. Toting chairs and blankets, music lovers arrived early on this balmy evening in July. The festival was unique, as its organizers were committed to airing new or unusual works. That summer, under an aqua, gold, and navy tent, attendees were treated to a full stage production of Strauss's *Ariadne auf Naxos* and a production of Stravinsky's *Oedipus Rex*, conducted by Leopold Stokowski.

Artists. In the early 1970s, the PIPC sponsored an artists-in-residence program. Talented young artists were housed in Harriman State Park for the summer while creating pieces for public display. Above, sculptor Hank DeRicco finishes his *Bitter Sweet Boogie Woogie*. Below, an unidentified painter discusses his work with a group of admirers. The PIPC continues the legacy of encouraging artists through its Artists in the Parks program.

Seven

TRAILS

Inviting in any season, they can be rocky and dry, smooth and straight, puddled and muddy, layered in crunchy crimson leaves, or powdered with sparkling snow. These are the over 250 miles of beautiful trails that wind through Harriman State Park. Hiking at the turn of the 20th century became popular worldwide. As early as 1920, Major Welch expressed a strong commitment "to make our park more usable to pedestrians and tramping organizations." To this end he met with representatives of walking societies such as the Appalachian Mountain Club, the Fresh Air Club, and the Green Mountain Club along with journalist and hiking enthusiast Raymond Torrey to solicit expert advice and to help build and maintain a network of trails throughout PIPC parklands. By enlisting the cooperation of interested, committed organizations, Welch laid the groundwork for generations of trail volunteers who have devoted their time and energy to planning, building, marking, and repairing the trails. A large portion of the work has been carried on under the auspices of the New York-New Jersey Trail Conference.

A sampling of the trails that traverse Harriman State Park includes a 25-mile section of the Long Path that starts at the George Washington Bridge and ends near Albany; the Kakiat Trail that runs east to west from the Ramapo River to the Mahwah River; the Ramapo-Dunderberg Trail, the first trail designed by Major Welch and executed by volunteers from the New York hiking clubs; and the 1779 Trail that roughly follows the route taken by Maj. Anthony Wayne in his surprise attack against the British at Stony Point. The most famous trail within the park is, of course, the Appalachian Trail (AT), the vision of Benton MacKaye, who imagined a great walking trail from Maine to Georgia. In fact, the first segment of the AT was constructed in Harriman Park stretching west to east from the Ramapo River to Bear Mountain and the Hudson River. This section opened on October 7, 1923. These days, a half million hikers traverse the AT through Harriman and Bear Mountain State Parks every year. Considered one of the most popular sections of the AT, wear and tear on the trail has caused serious erosion and necessitated relocating it six times. Currently crews are at work on a magnificent granite stairway on the eastern side of Bear Mountain, which they hope will be the last relocation.

Trails. There is a remarkable network of trails woven through Harriman State Park. Two thirds of them are marked and blazed according to the New York State Conservation Department. Generally red blazes are for east-west trails, blue for north-south, and yellow for diagonal. The Appalachian Trail is blazed in white. Additionally there are about 100 miles of unmarked trails.

Overnight Hike. An overnight hike to a remote location was part of the group camp experience. Cheerfully waving good-bye, the Girls Scouts of Camp Manhattan embark upon their "overnight" in 1926. They are carrying bedrolls tied securely over their shoulders. Wrapped in the bedrolls were blankets, towels, and perhaps a change of clothes.

Forty-Mile Hike. After a three-day hike, 50 campers of the Brooklyn Industrial School for Destitute Children hiked back to their camp along Seven Lakes Drive. Their trek covered 40 miles.

Mule Train. Eight hikers are pictured ascending one of Harriman's many mountains with the help of two pack mules. In the 1920s, hikers occasionally made use of pack animals on multi-night treks into the backcountry.

Trail Shelters. A front view, above, and rear view, below, of a typical trail shelter are seen in these two photographs. In 1927, Major Welch designed a rustic shelter that became the prototype for 16 others throughout the park. PIPC crews built them from logs, boulders, and flat slabs of granite a short distance from the main trails. An additional shelter on Stockbridge Mountain was created from a cave.

Break Time. Pictured above, four hikers prepare to make camp at Fingerboard Shelter atop Fingerboard Mountain. Below, eight adventurers pause for a rest and a hot lunch at the summit of a mountain around 1933. Sporting woolen knickers, the height of outdoor fashion, the ladies interrupted their hike at one of the stone and log shelters that existed throughout the park.

STICK FIGURES. These young ladies have mastered the classic outdoor cooking technique of barbecuing food on the end of a sharp stick. Along with marshmallows, hot dogs, and s'mores, the "doughboy" was a popular menu item. It consisted of biscuit dough wrapped around the end of a thick stick and baked over the flames until golden brown. The large pot being heated probably contains water for doing the dishes.

GO LEFT YOUNG MAN. Carrying heavy packs, four hikers pose by a camp directory before starting out. Judging from the sign, a left turn would be the better choice. Summit, Barnes, and the Twin Lakes were generally reserved for girls' camps.

Beech Trail. Hiker Peter Clark pauses on the Beech Trail near Tiorati Brook. One of the newer trails, it was blazed in 1972 by volunteers from the Westchester Trails Association and the New York-New Jersey Trail Conference. This trail encompasses many aspects of the history and evolution of the park. Hiking it, one sees Lake Welch, St. John's in the Wilderness Church, ruins of old farms, a woods road, a cemetery, and a picturesque park road. (Coffey collection.)

Stahahe (1920). Three hikers rest on the crest of Stahahe High Peak overlooking Lake Stahahe. The peak is accessible via a trail that ascended from the camp road. Visible below is the perimeter of Car Pond, the original body of water. It was enlarged in 1918 and increased from 17 to 88 acres.

Appalachian Trail. These trail workers, along with many colleagues from the New York-New Jersey Trail Conference, have recently completed a new section of the Appalachian Trail that was relocated due to erosion. The very first segment of the historic trail extended from the Elk Pen at Arden on the Ramapo River to the Hudson River at Bear Mountain. The work being done in these photographs is the building of granite stairs on a steep section of the trail on the east side of Bear Mountain. Using ancient methods of stonecutting and a system of pulleys, the steps have been painstakingly quarried, shaped, and set into place. Representing 6,000 hours of volunteer labor, the staircase is intended to be a durable, sustainable trail segment in harmony with the mountain. At left, volunteer Allegra Matthew wields a sledgehammer as she crushes granite to fill in a crib wall. Pictured below, crew leader Chris Ingui shapes a step using a hammer and chisel. (Both, courtesy New York-New Jersey Trail Conference.)

Eight

Nature Education

Early in its history, educating visitors about the wilderness became an important part of the PIPC's mission. An annual report published by the PIPC dates the beginning of nature education in Harriman Park to 1921. "The Boy Scouts began in this season a feature of nature education . . . by which natural objects of geology, botany, zoology, and entomology, are identified in place and studied under natural conditions. This work was initiated by Dr. Benjamin Talbot Babbitt Hyde of the American Museum of Natural History (AMNH) and was immediately extended to the 45 camps throughout the preserve." Along with exposure to exhibits and nature trails, campers were taken on day trips to the Arden side of the park to the insect study station under the auspices of Dr. Frank E. Lutz, curator of insect life at AMNH. Campers also visited the nature museums at Bear Mountain's Trailside Museums and Zoo. "In 1927," stated that year's *Palisades Interstate Park Commission Annual Report*, "nature councilors were employed to stimulate interest among camp directors and their charges." Soon there were satellite nature museums in four locations throughout the park: Lakes Kanawauke, Stahahe, and Tiorati and Twin Lakes. These attractive stone buildings constructed by the Works Progress Administration in the late 1920s still exist. Techniques used by nature educators emphasized the joy inherent in being a part of the wilderness. Children were taught to carefully handle and feed snakes and small mammals. Identification of trees, rocks, birds, animal tracks, insects, and small plants also formed part of the outdoor curriculum. An appreciation of the Native American heritage associated with the park was developed through special programs. One presenter was Princess Te Ata, a Cherokee Indian storyteller. The staff of the regional museums engaged in scientific research along with the performance of their teaching duties. In 1979, for example, they conducted a vegetation survey on pieces of the floating island of Lake Tiorati. During the 1970s, Bank Street College created the Tiorati Workshop, a highly successful training program for science teachers. Through its Trailside Regional Nature Museums program, the PIPC still continues the legacy of nature education into the present.

Uncle Benny. Scoutmaster Dr. Benjamin Hyde, known as "Uncle Bennie," demonstrates the proper handling of a snake to some fascinated campers. Hyde, who ran the children's corner of the American Museum of Natural History, was a naturalist, explorer, and founder of nature education in the park. Through collections and presentations, he provided meaningful encounters with the natural world. His exciting lectures were illustrated with lantern slides. Campers were taught to respect, rather than fear, wildlife.

Nature Exhibits. By 1921, the Boy Scouts had begun to include serious nature education as part of the camp experience. These on-site exhibits were a visually engaging way to introduce the basics of geology, biology, botany, zoology, and entomology. Created under the direction of Dr. Hyde, the nature programs became a fixture at all the camps, later developing into more formal museums housed in permanent buildings.

MUSEUM CABIN. This vintage postcard shows the museum cabin at Lower Twin Lake around 1922. It was utilized by Camp Manhattan, which was operated by the Girl Scouts of America. The rustic museum cabins were the predecessors of the sturdy stone structures built later by the Works Progress Administration (WPA) teams. Below, some of the camp's fearless young ladies assembled at the museum for a biology lesson on the care and feeding of snakes.

Bees. The behavior of bees was a topic of nature education at Camp Prospect during the 1920s. Wearing head nets, several campers stand near a hive on the roof of the mess hall of the converted Lewis house near Upper Twin Lake. The YWCA of Brooklyn operated the camp.

Teepee. A canvas teepee was erected to serve as the nature study venue for the Girl Scouts of Camp Paterson in 1923. Along certain trails, items of interest were labeled to draw the attention of hikers and help them learn by seeing and experiencing nature firsthand. These young ladies appear to be bird-watching. More than 230 species of birds have been identified in Harriman State Park.

Nature Museums. The impressive stone building above at Lake Kanawauke was the first formal nature museum in the park. Dr. Hyde established it. The interior contained wildlife displays consisting of tanks with snakes, fish, and other small animals in temporary captivity. By 1925, there were three more museums at Twin Lakes, Cohasset, and Tiorati, seen below. Educators working at these venues continue to inspire 6,000 campers annually with love of the natural world and environmental awareness. (Above, PIPC; below, Coffey collection.)

BULLETIN BOARD. Boy Scouts and their leaders read notices related to upcoming activities posted at headquarters. Along with rules of behavior, there were notices of nature programs on stargazing and animal tracking. Star talks were given on the dock as campers lay on their backs looking up at the night sky. One adult visitor reported hearing a little boy exclaim, "You can't look at the stars like this in the city. You'd get run over!"

PRINCESS TE ATA. Mary Thompson, a Chickasaw Indian princess, sits beside a stream observing a fawn. A graduate of Oklahoma College for Women, she was a trained actress and interpreter of Native American songs, dances, and stories. Under the name of Princess Te Ata, she performed at camps in the park from 1929 to 1946. During that time, she became acquainted with Eleanor Roosevelt and was invited to perform for guests of Franklin D. Roosevelt while he was governor. In 1942, while FDR was president, Thompson performed at the White House.

Storytelling. Children's group camps regularly provided entertainment in the evening. Part of nature education was an awareness of the history of Native Americans in the park. This performer was part of the Native American music and storytelling program in the mid-1900s.

Awards. At the conclusion of a camp session, awards were often given for nature projects such as displays, exhibits, and notebooks featuring leaves, ferns, and flowers with brief descriptions. The girls of Camp Kittredge on Upper Twin Lake gathered in 1925 for the presentation of prizes.

Tiorati Workshop. Nature educator Bettison Shapiro was surrounded by students and educators near Lake Tiorati in 1977. Shapiro was associated with the PIPC's Trailside Museums. In 1976, he developed the Tiorati Workshop for training teachers in environmental studies. After hands-on experiences among the bogs and lakes, teachers returned to their classrooms more skilled in natural sciences. Three times a year they brought their classes to Harriman State Park for field study. (Courtesy of Tiorati Workshop.)

Museum Interior. This is a view of the interior of the Twin Lakes Nature Museum. The young female campers move from one exhibit to another, observing the representations of various habitats. Typically nature counselors captured fish, snakes, frogs, and turtles at the beginning of the season and released them at the end of the summer.

Nine

SERVICE

For the last 100 years, both volunteer and professional groups and individuals have given their hard work and expertise for the creation and betterment of the park. The Palisades Interstate Park Police force began with patrolmen enforcing regulations about campfires, rubbish disposal, and rowdy behavior. It evolved into a highly trained force of professionals, including expert marksmen and scuba divers. Police patrols have always assisted motorists and park users, enforced laws, maintained safety and security at the park and the camps, conducted criminal investigations, and provided emergency road services. Initially they also served as the fire department and ambulance squad. Police utilized helicopters to aid in fire prevention, search and rescue, traffic control, and insuring the safety of campers. Beginning in the 1930s, rangers helped manage and protect wildlife. Nuisance animals were caught and relocated. During one hard winter, deer were fed to prevent starvation. Through the years, a skilled staff of PIPC employees built, rebuilt, and continue to maintain the complex infrastructure of the park and all the camps, roads, boats, docks, garages, and support facilities. They were involved in landscaping in public areas and replacing structures as they deteriorated. Highly trained professionals such as engineers, forestry experts, doctors, nurses, chefs, photographers, naturalists, and historians have contributed their talents to the park as well. Initially many park employees were former residents. Today their children and grandchildren carry on the tradition of working for the park.

Notable are the historic and ongoing efforts of volunteer trail workers. Along with the massive undertaking of the first segment of the Appalachian Trail in 1923 was the creation of numerous marked trails maintained by volunteers, many of who are members of the New York-New Jersey Trail Conference. Their constant efforts include repairing and rebuilding paths and bridges along with monitoring and preventing erosion.

In the discussion of service, it is important to acknowledge the generations of farsighted women and men, past, present, and future that are responsible in myriad ways for preserving the natural beauty and cultural significance of the parkland and open spaces.

Among them are members of the Palisades Park Conservancy, which works to promote and expand the preservation of natural, historical, and cultural resources in the park for the benefit of the public.

No Fishing. In an effort to protect depleted species, the PIPC posted a "No Hunting or Fishing" policy at certain locations. To make the point, a photographer snapped this amusing shot of police officer Leroy Taggart warning a would-be fisherman.

Police Force. Chief William Gee of the Palisades Interstate Park Police sits at center surrounded by fellow officers in front of their headquarters at Bear Mountain in 1919. The building was on the current site of the Bear Mountain Ice Skating Rink. The *Palisades Interstate Park Commission Annual Report 1924* noted that the summer force had increased to 36 patrolmen tasked with maintaining "an absolutely clean, orderly, and wholesome moral atmosphere" in every part of the park.

Police At Work. Lt. W. Alu, left, and two fellow officers of the Palisades Interstate Park Police Department attend to reports at their headquarters at Hessian Lodge around 1927. Police patrols assisted motorists and park users, enforced laws, maintained safety and security at the park and the camps, conducted criminal investigations, and provided emergency road services, services still carried on into the present.

Park Rangers. As a young man, Gerald Stalter, left, joined the park as a ranger under Chief William Gee. Originally a resident of Johnsontown, he later became the foreman of the 14 Kanawauke camps and moved his family to the stone foreman's cabin there. Pictured around 1937 are, from left to right, Stalter, unidentified, James Hurley, Edward "Muzz" Jones, and William Lawrence. (Stalter collection.)

Fourth of July. In 1940, a Fourth of July party was given for park police and employees at the Masonic Camp at Lake Kanawauke. They are pictured sitting on the lawn in front of the guesthouse, formerly owned by Joseph Shenstone, beside a table decorated in red, white, and blue. Police patrolled the camps constantly, and this picnic was a way of showing appreciation.

Policemen's Ball. The Policemen's Ball was an eagerly anticipated annual party in the 1940s. Held at the Bear Mountain Skating Rink, it was the social event of the year for police and rangers. Dancers could swing to the lilting sounds of famous bands hired for the evening. The charge was $1 per person. (Wallace collection.)

Stocking Trout. Park policemen look on as two workers stock trout at Lake Ascoti in 1962. Restocking the park's bodies of water was well documented in early park reports. Brook, rainbow, and brown trout, yellow perch, and smallmouth bass are among species placed in lakes and streams every year.

Fire Tower. Reached by an old woods road up Diamond Mountain, this fire tower was one of six in the park. Originally at the summit of Bear Mountain, it was removed in 1934 after Perkins Memorial Tower was built. It was relocated to Diamond Mountain in 1935.

MAINTENANCE. Park foreman Arthur Pohl at left, and Robert Doherty, maintenance man, remove siding from a mess hall at Upper Lake Cohasset around 1968. From the beginning, the camps required maintenance, improvement, and rebuilding. Gradually the number of camps has decreased to 32, and structures such as these were relocated or their parts were used to repair remaining buildings.

PARK WORKERS. Two unidentified park employees operated this specially equipped ice hoist near Tiorati Dam in January 1925. Ice harvesting took place on several lakes. Park employees were involved in numerous construction projects, including roads, icehouses, camps, pavilions, boathouses, shelters, garages, and dormitories.

CEDAR PONDS CABIN. Known originally as Cedar Ponds Cabin, this structure was built in 1925 at Lake Tiorati. It housed members of the park engineer's staff, some of whom are pictured in the foreground with skis, axe, snowshoes, and rifles. During the 1930s, the cabin was sided with stone. Today it serves as the group camp office.

BEAR MOUNTAIN CHEFS. In the early 1920s, a few camps prepared their own food in the mess halls, but the majority of hot meals were cooked at the Bear Mountain Inn and delivered to camps in automobiles outfitted with insulated containers. In 1925, the inn's chefs cooked more than 76,000 meals at a charge of 24¢ each.

Memory Keeper. Writer and former park resident Elizabeth "Perk" Stalter is seen guiding a walking tour through the Sandyfield cemetery to a group from the Historical Society of the Palisades Park Region. The society preserves archives, maintains cemeteries, and prepares educational exhibits. Author of *Doodletown*, Stalter enjoys sharing her extensive knowledge of the lost hamlets and the community of park employees. (Coffey collection.)

Trail Worker. The importance of trail workers in the parks cannot be overestimated. Volunteers clear fallen trees, debris, and trash. They relocate paths that become unsafe or eroded, maintain blazes, and make maps. Pictured is crew leader Kevin Spies with a rock saw, building stairs for the newly relocated segment of the Appalachian Trail. He embodies the words of writer George Lehmberg. "Now it is the responsibility of all of us to maintain and preserve this natural wonderland for future generations." (Courtesy New York-New Jersey Trail Conference.)

BIBLIOGRAPHY

Binnewiess, Robert O. *Palisades: 100,000 Acres in 100 Years*. New York: Fordham University Press, 2001.

Dann, Kevin. *Across the Great Border Fault: The Naturalist Myth in America*. New Brunswick, NJ: Rutgers University Press, 2000.

Elliott, Odessa. *That Much Good Might Be Done*. Kearny, NJ: Morris Publishing, 2002.

Figliomeni, Michelle. *E. H. Harriman at Arden Farms*. Washingtonville, NY: Spear Printing, Inc., 1997.

Focht, Jack., ed. *Trailside Papers*. Bear Mountain, NY.

Howell, William Thompson. *The Hudson Highlands*. New York: Walking News, 1982.

Lenik, Edward. *Iron Mine Trails*. New York, NY: NY-NJ Trail Conference, 1996.

Mastrodonato, Alfred. *My Days at Pine Meadow CCC Camp*. Palisades Interstate Park Commission *Trailside Papers: H-08/99*. Bear Mountain, NY, 1999.

Myles, William J. *Harriman Trails*. New York: New York–New Jersey Trail Conference, 1991.

Muir, John. *Edward Henry Harriman*. Garden City, NY: Doubleday and Company, 1912.

Palisades Interstate Park Commission Annual Reports 1900–1929. Bear Mountain, NY: PIPC.

Ransom, James M. *Vanishing Ironworks of the Ramapos*. New Brunswick, NJ: Rutgers University Press, 1966.

Salomon, Julian Harris. *Indians of the Lower Hudson Region: The Munsee*. New City, NY: Historical Society of Rockland County, 1982.

Sixty Years of Park Cooperation. Report of the PIPC 1900–1960. Bear Mountain: New York, 1961.

Smith, Andrew. "The Lost Towns." *Rockland County: Century of History*. Ed. by Linda Zimmerman. New City, NY: Historical Society of Rockland County, 2000.

Consistent with our mission to preserve history on a local level, this book was printed in South Carolina on American-made paper and manufactured entirely in the United States. Products carrying the accredited Forest Stewardship Council (FSC) label are printed on 100 percent FSC-certified paper.

MADE IN THE USA